D1520119

EXPLORE THE UNITED STATES

PUERTO RICO

Sarah Tieck

Big Buddy Books

An Imprint of Abdo Publishing
abdobooks.com

abdobooks.com

Published by Abdo Publishing, a division of ABDO, PO Box 398166, Minneapolis, Minnesota 55439. Copyright © 2020 by Abdo Consulting Group, Inc. International copyrights reserved in all countries. No part of this book may be reproduced in any form without written permission from the publisher. Big Buddy Books™ is a trademark and logo of Abdo Publishing.

Printed in the United States of America, North Mankato, Minnesota
102019
012020

THIS BOOK CONTAINS
RECYCLED MATERIALS

Design: Aruna Rangarajan, Mighty Media, Inc.
Production: Mighty Media, Inc.
Editor: Liz Salzmann

Cover Photograph: Shutterstock Images
Interior Photographs: 97/iStockphoto, p. 29 (bottom left); Alamy Photo, p. 13; AP Images, p. 21; Brennan Linsley/AP Images, p. 27; cdwheatley/iStockphoto, p. 5; David Villafane/Staff/AP Images, p. 20; demerzel21/iStockphoto, p. 24; dennisvdw/iStockphoto, p. 29 (bottom right); E_Rojas/iStockphoto, p. 30 (middle); Gilberto Villasana/iStockphoto, p. 30 (top); HaraldEWeiss/iStockphoto, p. 16; Henry Mestre/Flickr, p. 9 (bottom right); jrroman/iStockphoto, p. 28 (middle); Nick Lisi/AP Images, p. 19; OGphoto/iStockphoto, p. 15; Shutterstock Images, pp. 7, 9, 10, 11, 17, 18, 23, 25, 26, 28, 29, 30; Southern Methodist University/Library of Congress, p. 26 (top right); US Department of Defense/Wikimedia Commons, p. 27 (bottom); Wikimedia Commons, p. 9 (top left); WMarissen/iStockphoto, p. 30 (bottom)

Populations figures from census.gov

Library of Congress Control Number: 2019943514

Publisher's Cataloging-in-Publication Data
Names: Tieck, Sarah, author.
Title: Puerto Rico / by Sarah Tieck
Description: Minneapolis, Minnesota : Abdo Publishing, 2020 | Series: Explore the United States | Includes online resources and index.
Identifiers: ISBN 9781532191428 (lib. bdg.) | ISBN 9781532178153 (ebook)
Subjects: LCSH: U.S. states--Juvenile literature. | Puerto Rico--Relations--United States--Juvenile literature. | Physical geography--United States--Juvenile literature. | Puerto Rico--History--Juvenile literature.
Classification: DDC 972.95--dc23

CONTENTS

ONE NATION

The United States is a diverse country. It has farmland, cities, coasts, and mountains. Its people come from many different backgrounds. And, its history covers more than 200 years.

Puerto Rico (PAWR-tuh REE-koh) became a US territory in 1898. It became a US commonwealth in 1952. Let's learn more about Puerto Rico and its story!

Puerto Rico is known for its beautiful beaches.

CHAPTER 2

PUERTO RICO UP CLOSE

Puerto Rico is a US commonwealth. This means it is governed by its own people. But, Puerto Ricans are US citizens. So, they must follow most US laws. And, they can live in the United States if they choose.

Puerto Rico is a large island southeast of Florida. It also includes the nearby islands Mona, Culebra, and Vieques. The Atlantic Ocean is north. The Caribbean Sea is south.

Puerto Rico has a total area of 3,424 square miles (8,868 sq km). About 3.2 million people live there.

The Caribbean Islands

FLORIDA

Gulf of Mexico

THE BAHAMAS

ATLANTIC OCEAN

Turks & Caicos Islands

CUBA

DOMINICAN REPUBLIC

Virgin Islands

Cayman Islands

BELIZE

HAITI

JAMAICA

PUERTO RICO

HONDURAS

Caribbean Sea

NICARAGUA

N
W · E
S

7

CHAPTER 3

IMPORTANT CITIES

San Juan (san-WAHN) is Puerto Rico's capital. It is also the island's largest city, with 320,967 people. The city has walls and forts that were built beginning in the 1500s. It also has beaches and a busy port.

Bayamón (beye-ah-MOHN) is the second-largest city on the island. It is home to 170,480 people. It is part of the San Juan metropolitan area.

DID YOU KNOW?

Many people in Puerto Rico speak Spanish and English.

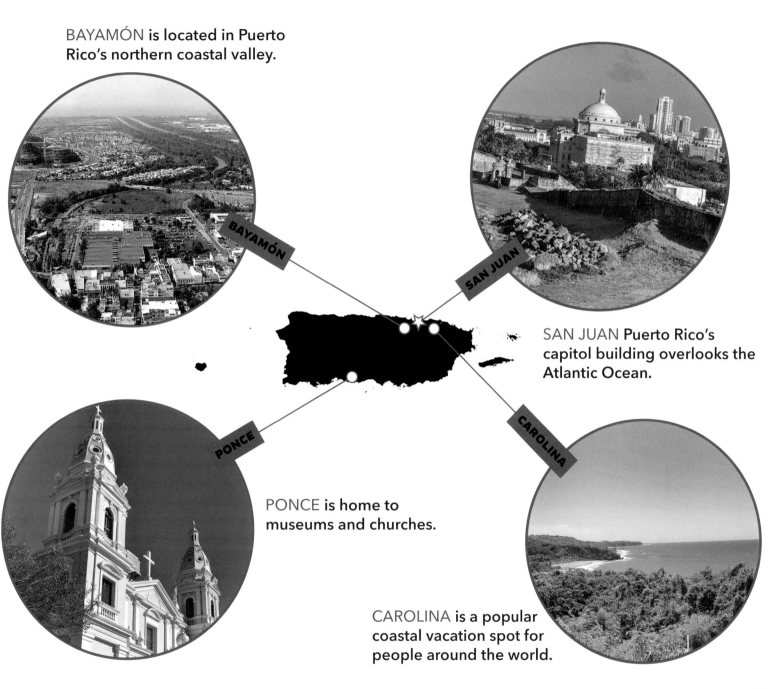

BAYAMÓN is located in Puerto Rico's northern coastal valley.

SAN JUAN Puerto Rico's capitol building overlooks the Atlantic Ocean.

PONCE is home to museums and churches.

CAROLINA is a popular coastal vacation spot for people around the world.

Carolina is Puerto Rico's third-largest city. It is home to 147,661 people. It features Plaza Carolina, one of the island's largest malls. The city is also home to hotels and beaches. It attracts many visitors.

Ponce (PAWN-say) is the island's fourth-largest city, with 133,191 people. It is known for business and the arts.

DID YOU KNOW?
Puerto Rico's governor lives in a building known as La Fortaleza. It is in a very old part of San Juan.

Parque de Bombas is a former fire station in Ponce. This well-known landmark is now a museum.

CHAPTER 4

PUERTO RICO IN HISTORY

Puerto Rico's history includes Native Americans and explorers. Before Europeans arrived, the Taino people lived on the land. They lived in villages and grew crops.

In 1493, explorer Christopher Columbus claimed the island for Spain. Spain ruled the island for more than 400 years.

After the Spanish-American War in 1898, Spain gave Puerto Rico to the United States. The island became a US commonwealth in 1952.

DID YOU KNOW?

Puerto Rico means "rich port" in Spanish.

Spanish explorer Juan Ponce de León became Puerto Rico's first governor in 1509.

CHAPTER 5

ACROSS THE LAND

Puerto Rico has beaches, hills, mountains, and forests. The Arecibo River flows from the mountains into the Atlantic Ocean. Orchids and other flowers grow on the island year-round.

The island has many types of birds. Bats, mongooses, and lizards also live there. Many kinds of fish are found in the island's coastal waters.

DID YOU KNOW?

Puerto Rico has mild weather all year. In July, the average temperature is 88.5°F (31.4°C). In January, it is 83.1°F (28.3°C)!

El Yunque National Forest is a rain forest in eastern Puerto Rico. It can get more than 200 inches (508 cm) of rain a year!

CHAPTER 6

EARNING A LIVING

Puerto Rico has important manufacturing businesses. People work in factories that make chemicals, food, and clothing.

The island's warm weather attracts visitors. So, many Puerto Ricans work for restaurants and hotels.

Puerto Rico's farms produce dairy and meat. Fruit, tobacco, and coffee beans are major crops.

DID YOU KNOW?

Many island visitors pass through Puerto Rico's three international airports. The largest airport is Luis Muñoz Marín International Airport.

Coffee beans grown in Puerto Rico are sold around the world.

CHAPTER 7

SPORTS PAGE

Many people think of baseball when they think of Puerto Rico. It is a popular sport on the island, along with soccer, boxing, and basketball. Also, Puerto Rico has been part of the Olympic Games since 1948.

DID YOU KNOW?

Tennis player Monica Puig was born in San Juan in 1993. She won the gold medal in women's singles at the 2016 Olympic Games.

Félix "Tito" Trinidad is considered one of the best Puerto Rican boxers. He entered the International Boxing Hall of Fame in 2014.

CHAPTER 8

HOMETOWN HEROES

Many famous people are from Puerto Rico. Baseball player Roberto Clemente was born in Carolina in 1934. He played baseball with the Pittsburgh Pirates from 1955 until his death in 1972. He won awards for his strong playing skills.

Politician Carmen Yulín Cruz was born in San Juan in 1963. She served in Congress and was elected mayor of San Juan in 2012. Cruz has won many awards and honors for her service to Puerto Rico.

After Hurricane Maria struck Puerto Rico in 2017, Cruz worked hard to help the commonwealth recover.

Clemente worked to help other Latin American baseball players. He wanted them to be treated fairly.

José Feliciano was born in Lares in 1945. His given name was José Montserrate Feliciano García. He grew up in New York City, New York.

Feliciano is a famous singer, songwriter, and guitar player. Feliciano was born blind. He taught himself to play the guitar as a child.

In 1970, Feliciano wrote a holiday song called "Feliz Navidad." This means "Merry Christmas" in Spanish. The song is still well-liked today.

In 2019, Feliciano was honored at New York City's Puerto Rican Day Parade.

CHAPTER 9

A GREAT PLACE

The story of Puerto Rico is important to the United States. The people and places that make up this commonwealth offer something special to the country. Together with the states, Puerto Rico helps make the United States great.

Many visitors go to Cave Window to look out over Puerto Rico. The cave is called *Cueva Ventana* in Spanish.

Forests cover the Cordillera Central mountains. The mountains include Cerro de Punta. At 4,390 feet (1,338 m), it is Puerto Rico's highest point.

TIMELINE

1873

Slavery was outlawed in Puerto Rico.

1917

Puerto Ricans became US citizens.

1940

An important US military base called **Fort** Buchanan was built in San Juan.

1800s

Puerto Rico became known for growing sugarcane and coffee beans. These crops were grown on large farms that used **slave** labor.

1830

Spain and the United States fought in the **Spanish-American War**. At its end, Puerto Rico became a territory of the United States.

1898

1952

Puerto Rico became a US **commonwealth** on July 25.

2011

President Barack Obama became the first US president to make an official visit to Puerto Rico since 1961.

1900s

2000s

Puerto Rico took part in the Olympic Games for the first time.

1948

Sila María Calderón became Puerto Rico's first female governor.

2001

Hurricane Maria struck Puerto Rico. Nearly 3,000 people were killed and many buildings were ruined. It was considered to be the worst natural disaster to affect Puerto Rico.

2017

TOUR BOOK

Do you want to go to Puerto Rico? If you visit the island, here are some places to go and things to do!

SEE
Go into the caverns of Rio Camuy Cave Park near Arecibo. They have one of the world's largest underground rivers.

Arroz con gandules is often served with Puerto Rican style roast pork called pernil.

TASTE
Try some *arroz con gandules*. This famous rice dish is a Puerto Rican specialty.

EXPLORE

Visit Old San Juan. This walled part of San Juan is known for its historic buildings. Many people shop there.

See Old San Juan's Spanish forts, such as Castillo San Cristóbal.

PLAY

Visit one of Puerto Rico's sandy beaches. Splash in the ocean waves or pick up seashells!

DISCOVER

See San Juan Bay from historic El Morro. This famous fort was built by the Spanish between 1539 and 1787.

FAST FACTS

▸ FLAG:

▸ FLOWER
Flor de Maga
(Puerto Rican
Hibiscus)

▸ NICKNAME:
Isle of Enchantment

▸ DATE OF BECOMING A
US COMMONWEALTH:
July 25, 1952

▸ POPULATION:
3,195,153

▸ TREE
Ceiba Tree
(Silk-Cotton Tree)

▸ TOTAL AREA:
3,424 square miles

▸ CAPITAL:
San Juan

▸ BIRD
Reina Mora
(Puerto Rican
Spindalis)

▸ POSTAL ABBREVIATION:
PR

▸ MOTTO:
"Joannes est nomen ejus"
(John Is His Name)

GLOSSARY

capital—a city where government leaders meet.

commonwealth—a nation, state, or other political unit governed by its own people. It is united with another country.

diverse—made up of things that are different from each other.

fort—a building with strong walls to guard against enemies.

hurricane—a tropical storm that forms over seawater with strong winds, rain, thunder, and lightning.

metropolitan—of or relating to a large city, usually with nearby smaller cities called suburbs.

slave—a person who is bought and sold as property.

Spanish-American War—a war fought between the United States and Spain in 1898.

ONLINE RESOURCES

Booklinks
NONFICTION NETWORK
FREE! ONLINE NONFICTION RESOURCES

To learn more about Puerto Rico, please visit **abdobooklinks.com** or scan this QR code. These links are routinely monitored and updated to provide the most current information available.

INDEX